PRACTICE PROBLEMS AND CASE STUDY

TO ACCOMPANY

The Financial Management of Hospitals and Healthcare Organizations

PRACTICE PROBLEMS AND CASE STUDY

TO ACCOMPANY

The Financial Management of Hospitals and Healthcare Organizations

Michael Nowicki

AUPHA

12   11   10   09   08   5   4   3   2   1

Library of Congress Cataloging-in-Publication Data

Nowicki, Michael.
   Practice problems and case study to accompany the financial management of hospitals and healthcare organizations / Michael Nowicki.
      p.cm.
   ISBN-13: 978-1-56793-284-3 (alk. paper)
   ISBN-10: 1-56793-284-3 (alk. paper)
      1. Hospitals--Business management--Problems, exercises, etc. 2. Hospitals--Finance--Problems, exercises, etc. 3. Health facilities--Business management--Problems, exercises, etc. 4. Health facilities--Finance--Problems, exercises, etc. I. Title.

   RA971.3.N693 2008
   362.11068--dc22

                                                                      2007031437

Acquisitions editor: Janet Davis; project manager: Amanda Bove; Designer: Chris Underdown

Health Administration Press
A division of the Foundation of the
   American College of Healthcare Executives
1 North Franklin Street, Suite 1700
Chicago, IL 60606-3434
(312) 424-2800

CONTENTS

INSTRUCTIONS AND ACKNOWLEDGMENTS

I developed this book of practice problems as a supplement to *The Financial Management of Hospitals and Healthcare Organizations* in response to student requests for more problems to practice and a case in which they could apply the problems. For each quantitative concept, I developed three problems: (1) an in-class problem and detailed solution found in the textbook; (2) a practice problem and detailed solution found in this workbook; (3) and a self-quiz problem with solution found in the back of this workbook.

Although instructors will most often work the in-class problem during class, students should attempt to solve the problems on their own while they prepare for class. Students should attempt to solve the practice problems after class and compare their answers to the practice problem solutions. When students have difficulty solving the practice problem, they should seek the assistance of their instructors. While students are studying for tests, they should attempt the self-quiz problem to determine if they have remembered and mastered the concept. Again, when students have difficulty solving the self-quiz problem, they should seek the assistance of their instructors.

Because mastering these problems takes practice, I believe that students should try to develop their own, additional practice problems to better understand the concepts. Not only will developing additional practice problems give students extra practice, but it will also give students insight on how instructors prepare problems for tests.

The problems regarding ratios relate to the financial statements found in Chapter 14 of the textbook. Those financial statements and notes were provided by the 2006 edition of *HFMA's Introduction to Hospital Accounting,* and I would like to acknowledge and thank the HFMA for permission to use the material.

In addition to the practice problems, I have provided a comprehensive case so that students can apply what they've learned to a practical "real-world" setting. The case method instructions were adapted from *Cases in Health Services Management,* and I gratefully acknowledge and thank its authors: Jonathan S. Rakich, Indiana University Southeast; Beaufort B. Longest, University of Pittsburg; and one of my favorite professors and mentors, Kurt Darr, The George Washington University.

—Michael Nowicki, Ed.D., FACHE, FHFMA
Professor and Director
School of Health Administration
Texas State University

COST SHIFTING/COST CUTTING

Cost-Shifting Practice Problem

Next year, XYZ Healthcare Organization will serve 100 patients analyzed in the following manner:

    20 Medicare patients, who pay $950 per diagnosis
    30 Medicaid patients, who pay $900 per diagnosis
    25 managed care patients, who pay charges minus a 15% discount
    10 managed care patients, who pay charges minus a 25% discount
     5 private insurance patients, who pay charges
     5 charity care patients, who pay nothing
     5 bad debt patients, who pay nothing

Next year, XYZ's costs will be $1,000 per patient. Calculate the charge necessary to recover XYZ's cost.

	No	Costs	Charges	Collection	Profit
medicare	20	20,000	20000	19,000	-1000
medicaid	30	30,000	30,000	27,000	-3000
manged care#1	25	25,000	25000	21,250	-3750
mc #2	10	10000	10000	7500	-2500
private	5	5000	5000	5000	0
charity	5	5000	5000	0	-5000
Bad debt	5	5000	5000	0	-5000
	100	100,000	100,000	79,750	-20,250

$$\frac{20,250}{25(.85)+10(.75)+5} + 1000 = X$$

$$\frac{20,250}{21.25+7.5+5} + 1000 = X$$

$$\frac{20,250}{33.75} + 1000 = X$$

$$600 + 1000 = X$$

$$1600 = X$$

Cost-Shifting Practice Problem Solution

Step 1: Calculate the total projected loss by assuming the charge per patient equals the cost per patient.

Payer	No.	Costs ($)	Charges ($)	Collections ($)	Profit ($)
Medicare	20	20,000	20,000	19,000	−1,000
Medicaid	30	30,000	30,000	27,000	−3,000
MC #1	25	25,000	25,000	21,250	−3,750
MC #2	10	10,000	10,000	7,500	−2,500
Private insurance	5	5,000	5,000	5,000	0
Charity	5	5,000	5,000	0	−5,000
Bad debt	5	5,000	5,000	0	−5,000
Total	100	100,000	100,000	79,750	−20,250

Step 2: Calculate the charge necessary to recover XYZ's cost by dividing the loss by the number of patients who will pay an increased charge, or portion thereof, and then add the cost per patient to the answer.

$$\frac{\$20,250}{25(.85) + 10(.75) + 5} + \$1,000 = \$1,600$$

Step 3: Check the answer by calculating the profit/loss using the new charge.

Payer	No.	Costs ($)	Charges ($)	Collections ($)	Profit ($)
Medicare	20	20,000	32,000	19,000	−1,000
Medicaid	30	30,000	48,000	27,000	−3,000
MC #1	25	25,000	40,000	34,000	9,000
MC #2	10	10,000	16,000	12,000	2,000
Private insurance	5	5,000	8,000	8,000	3,000
Charity	5	5,000	8,000	0	−5,000
Bad debt	5	5,000	8,000	0	−5,000
Total	100	100,000	160,000	100,000	0

Cost-Cutting Practice Problem

Using the practice problem on cost shifting, assume that those payers that pay charges, or charges minus a discount, limit XYZ's charges to $1,050 per patient. Calculate the amount of costs that XYZ will need to cut, or cover with additional revenues, to break even (realize no profit or loss).

	NO	Cost	Charges	Collection	Profit
Medicare	20	20000	21,000	19000	-1000
Medicaid	30	30000	31,500	27000	-3000
mc #1	25	25000	26,250	22313	-2687
mc #2	10	10000	10,500	7875	-2125
Private	5	5000	5250	5250	250
Charity	5	5000	5250	0	-5000
Bad debt	5	5000	5250	0	-5000
	100	100,000	105000	81438	-18562

$$\frac{100000 - 18562}{100} = X \qquad \frac{81438}{100} = X \qquad 814.38 = X$$

Cost-Cutting Practice Problem Solution

Step 1: Calculate the total costs to be cut by using the new charge per patient to determine the profit/loss.

Payer	No.	Costs ($)	Charges ($)	Collections ($)	Profit ($)
Medicare	20	20,000	21,000	19,000	−1,000
Medicaid	30	30,000	31,500	27,000	−3,000
MC #1	25	25,000	26,250	22,313	−2,687
MC #2	10	10,000	10,500	7,875	−2,125
Private insurance	5	5,000	5,250	5,250	250
Charity	5	5,000	5,250	0	−5,000
Bad debt	5	5,000	5,250	0	−5,000
Total	100	100,000	105,000	81,438	−18,562

Step 2: Check the answer by calculating the profit/loss using the new cost per patient:

$$\frac{\$100,000 - \$18,562}{100} = \$814.38$$

Payer	No.	Costs ($)	Charges ($)	Collections ($)	Profit ($)
Medicare	20	16,288	21,000	19,000	2,712
Medicaid	30	24,431	31,500	27,000	2,569
MC #1	25	20,360	26,250	22,313	1,953
MC #2	10	8,144	10,500	7,875	−269
Private insurance	5	4,072	5,250	5,250	1,178
Charity	5	4,072	5,250	0	−4,072
Bad debt	5	4,072	5,250	0	−4,072
Total	100	81,439	105,000	81,438	−1

Cost-Shifting Self-Quiz Problem

Assume your organization has 100 patients analyzed in the following manner:

15 Medicare patients, who pay $2,000 per diagnosis
25 Medicaid patients, who pay $1,800 per diagnosis
20 managed care patients, who pay charges minus a 20% discount
10 managed care patients, who pay charges minus a 25% discount
10 private insurance patients, who pay charges
10 charity care patients, who pay nothing
10 bad debt patients, who pay nothing

Your organization's average cost per patient is $2,000. Calculate the charge necessary to recover your cost.

	No	Cost	Charge	Collection	Profit
Medicare	15	30000	30000	30000	0
Medicaid	25	50000	50000	45000	−5000
mc #1	20	40000	40000	32000	−8000
mc #2	10	20000	20000	15000	−5000
Private	10	20000	20000	20000	0
Charity	10	20000	20000	0	−20000
Bad debt	10	20000	20000	0	−20000
		200,000	200,000	142,000	−58,000

$$\frac{58,000}{20(.80) + 10(.75) + 10} + 2000 = X \qquad \frac{58,000}{16 + 7.5 + 10} + 2000 = X \qquad \frac{58,000}{33.50} + 2000$$

$$1731 + 2000 = X$$

$$3731 = X$$

Cost-Cutting Self-Quiz Problem 3731

Using the data from the self-quiz problem on cost shifting, assume those who pay charges will allow a maximum charge of $2,100. Calculate the amount of costs you will need to cut to break even.

	NO	Cost	charge	collection	profit
					0
medicare	15	30000	31500	30000	-5000
medicaid	25	50000	52500	45000	
mc #1 (20%)	20	40000	42000	33600	6400
mc #2 (25%)	10	7000 0	21000	15750	-4250
			21000	21000	1000
Private	10	80000	21000	0	-20000
charity	10	80000	21000	0	-20000
Bad debt	10	90000	21000		
	100	200,000	210000	145350	-54650

$$\frac{200000 - 54650 -}{100}$$

$$\frac{145350}{100} = 1453.50$$

DIFFERENTIAL COST ANALYSIS

Differential Cost Analysis Practice Problem

Beta Managed Care Corporation has approached XYZ Hospital for inpatient labor and delivery coverage for Beta's subscribers. Beta will pay $5,000 per delivery. XYZ's fixed costs per delivery are $3,000, and variable costs are $3,000. Using differential cost analysis, should XYZ Hospital accept Beta's offer?

Differential Cost Analysis Practice Problem Solution

Step 1: Gather all costs and revenues associated with each alternative.

	Accept	Reject
Revenue	$ 5,000	$ 0
Fixed Cost	3,000	3,000
Variable Costs	3,000	0
Full Cost Gain/(Loss)	**($1,000)**	**($3,000)**

Step 2: Identify and drop all sunk costs (drop 3,000 fixed cost for each alternative).

	Accept	Reject
Revenue	$5,000	$0
Fixed Cost	0	0
Variable Costs	3,000	0

Step 3: Identify and drop all costs and revenues that do not differ between the alternatives.

	Accept	Reject
Revenue	$5,000	$0
Fixed Cost	0	0
Variable Costs	3,000	0

Step 4: Select the best alternative based on the remaining cost and revenue information.

	Accept	Reject
Revenue	$ 5,000	$0
Fixed Cost	0	0
Variable Costs	3,000	0
Differential Cost Gain/(Loss)	**$2,000**	**$0**

Conclusion: Using differential cost analysis, XYZ should accept the offer because it has a higher differential gain ($2,000) than rejecting the offer ($0).

Differential Cost Analysis Self-Quiz Problem

The integrated delivery system you work for is thinking about dropping your sleep disorder program for financial reasons. The program serves 4,000 patients a year with annual revenues of $2,000,000. The variable cost per patient is $200 with allocated fixed costs to the program of $1,600,000. Should your program be dropped for financial reasons?

	Keep	Drop
	Accept	Reject
Revenue	2,000,000	0
Fixed costs	1,600,000	1,600,000
Variable costs	800 000	0
	(−400,000)	(1,600,000)

Drop sunk costs

Rev	2,000,000	0
Fixed	0	0
Variable	800 000	0

Drop cost & Rev not different

Rev	2,000,000	0
Fixed	0	0
Variable	800 000	0

Select

Rev	2000 000	0
Fixed	0	0
Varible	800 000	0
	1,200,000	0

Should not drop program

JOB-ORDER COSTING

Job-Order Costing Practice Problem

XYZ Reference Lab must calculate the relative value and cost per procedure given that the total lab expense is $851,455:

Procedure	Projected Volume	Labor Expense ($)
A	4,000	.10
B	3,500	.05
C	2,000	.05
D	4,000	.15
E	4,500	.10
F	6,000	.10
G	2,200	.15
H	1,800	.15
I	4,000	.05
J	3,000	.10

Job-Order Costing Practice Problem Solution

Stage 1: Calculate RVUs by dividing labor expense per procedure by the average labor expense.

Procedure	Labor Expense ($)	÷	Average Labor Expense ($)	=	RVU
A	.10		.10		1.0
B	.05		.10		.5
C	.05		.10		.5
D	.15		.10		1.5
E	.10		.10		1.0
F	.10		.10		1.0
G	.15		.10		1.5
H	.15		.10		1.5
I	.05		.10		.5
J	.10		.10		1.0

Stage 2, Step 1: Calculate total RVUs by multiplying RVUs per procedure by projected volume.

Procedure	RVU	x	Projected Volume	=	Total RVUs
A	1.0		4,000		4,000
B	.5		3,500		1,750
C	.5		2,000		1,000
D	1.5		4,000		6,000
E	1.0		4,500		4,500
F	1.0		6,000		6,000
G	1.5		2,200		3,300
H	1.5		1,800		2,700
I	.5		4,000		2,000
J	1.0		3,000		3,000
					34,250

Stage 2, Step 2: Calculate the cost per RVU by dividing total costs by total RVUs.

$851,455 ÷ 34,250 = $24.86

Stage 2, Step 3: Calculate the cost per procedure by multiplying the cost per RVU by RVUs per procedure.

Procedure	Cost/RVU	x	RVUs/Procedure	=	Cost/Procedure
A	24.86		1.0		24.86
B	24.86		.5		12.43
C	24.86		.5		12.43
D	24.86		1.5		37.29
E	24.86		1.0		24.86
F	24.86		1.0		24.86
G	24.86		1.5		37.29
H	24.86		1.5		37.29
I	24.86		.5		12.43
J	24.86		1.0		24.86

Job-Order Costing Self-Quiz Problem

Using the weighted procedure method of setting rates, calculate the relative value and cost per procedure for the following lab procedures given a total lab cost of $1,250,000 and an average hourly lab tech rate of $15 (to calculate the RVU, divide the total sample expense by the common denominator of 5):

Procedure	Projected Volume	Labor in Minutes	Supply Expense ($)
Amylase	4,000	15	.75
Bleeding time	5,000	12	.60
Uric acid	3,000	10	.50
Platelet count	7,800	9	.40
Hematocrit	7,600	8	.35

Total sample expense / RVU / TOTA RVU

	Total sample expense	RVU	TOTA RVU
A	4.5	.90	3600
B	3.6	.72	3600
U	3	.60	1800
P	2.65	.53	4134
H	2.35	.47	3572
			16706

COST/RVU
74.82

Procedure	COST/RVU	RVU	COST/Prod
A	74.82	.90	67.34
B	74.82	.72	53.87
U	74.82	.60	44.89
P	74.82	.53	39.66
H	74.82	.47	31.17

ACTIVITY-BASED COSTING

Activity-Based Costing Practice Problem

XYZ Home Health Care Corporation wants to develop a product cost for the following home visits using labor expense and supply expense to assign direct costs and visit minutes as a cost driver to assign indirect costs. Projected total costs for the home health care corporation are $6,000,000 ($5,000,000 direct and $1,000,000 indirect). Assign costs to each visit using the following information:

Visit	Projected Volumes	Labor Expense ($)	Supply Expense ($)	Visit Minutes
Physical therapy (PT)	2,000	60	30	60
Respiratory therapy (RT)	4,000	50	20	40
Nursing	9,000	25	10	30
Occupational therapy (OT)	7,000	20	5	40

Activity-Based Costing Practice Problem Solution

Stage 1: Calculate the direct RVU and the indirect RVU for each visit.

Step 1: Divide total sample direct cost (labor expense + supply expense) by either the greatest common denominator (GCD) (if there is one) or the average sample direct cost for each visit.

Visit	Total Sample Direct Cost ($) ÷	GCD =	Direct RVU
PT	90	5	18
RT	70	5	14
Nursing	35	5	7
OT	25	5	5

Step 2: Divide total sample indirect cost (visit minutes) by either the GCD or the average sample indirect cost for each visit.

Visit	Total Sample Indirect Cost ($) ÷	GCD =	Indirect Cost Drivers
PT	60	10	6
RT	40	10	4
Nursing	30	10	3
OT	40	10	4

Stage 2: Calculate the total cost for each visit.

Step 1: Calculate the total projected direct RVUs by multiplying the direct RVUs per visit by the projected volume per visit.

Visit	RVU ×	Projected Volume =	Total Direct RVUs
PT	18	2,000	36,000
RT	14	4,000	56,000
Nursing	7	9,000	63,000
OT	5	7,000	35,000
			190,000

Step 2: Calculate the total projected indirect cost drivers by multiplying the indirect RVUs per visit by the projected volume per visit.

Visit	RVU	x	Projected Volume	=	Total Indirect Cost Drivers
PT	6		2,000		12,000
RT	4		4,000		16,000
Nursing	3		9,000		27,000
OT	4		7,000		28,000
					83,000

Step 3: Calculate the direct cost per RVU by dividing direct costs by total direct RVUs.

$5,000,000 ÷ 190,000 = $26.32

Step 4: Calculate the indirect cost per cost driver by dividing indirect costs by total indirect cost drivers.

$1,000,000 ÷ 83,000 = $12.05

Step 5: Calculate the direct cost per procedure by multiplying the direct cost per RVU by the direct RVUs in each procedure.

Visit	Direct Cost/RVU ($)	x	Direct RVU	=	Direct Cost/ Visit ($)
PT	26.32		18		473.76
RT	26.32		14		368.48
Nursing	26.32		7		184.24
OT	26.32		5		131.60

Step 6: Calculate the indirect cost per visit by multiplying the indirect cost per RVU by the indirect RVUs in each procedure.

Visit	Indirect Cost/RVU ($)	x Indirect Cost Driver =	Indirect Cost/Visit ($)
PT	12.05	6	72.30
RT	12.05	4	48.20
Nursing	12.05	3	36.15
OT	12.05	4	48.20

Step 7: Calculate the total cost per procedure by adding the direct cost per procedure and the indirect cost per procedure.

Visit	Direct Cost/Visit ($) +	Indirect Cost/Visit ($) =	Total Cost/Visit ($)
PT	473.76	72.30	546.06
RT	368.48	48.20	416.68
Nursing	184.24	36.15	220.39
OT	131.60	48.20	179.80

Activity-Based Costing Self-Quiz Problem

Your wellness clinic wants to develop a product cost for the following activities using labor expense and supply expense to assign direct costs and visit minutes as a cost driver to assign indirect costs. Projected total costs for your wellness clinic are $600,000 ($300,000 direct and $300,000 indirect). Assign costs to each activity using the following information:

Activity	Projected Volumes	Labor Expense ($)	Supply Expense ($)	RVU	Visit Minutes	IND. Cost Driver
Evaluation	4,000	30	10	40 8	60	6
Education	3,000	50	20	70 14	40	4
Exercise	2,000	05	00	5. 1	90	9

ACT	Projected Vol	X	RVU	=	TOTAL Direct RVU	3.95/RVU
EV	4000		8		32,000	
ED	3000		14		42,000	
EX	2000		1		2000	
					76000	

5.56/RVU

	INDIRECT COST DRIVER	Proj. VOL	=	TOTAL IND.
EV	6	4000		24,000
ED	4	3000		12000
EX	9	2000		18000
				54,000

Direct Cost	RVU	COST/RVU	COST/ACT
EV	8	3.95	31.60
ED	14	3.95	55.30
EX	1	3.95	3.95

Indirect cost			
EV	6	5.56	33.36
ED	4	5.56	22.24
EX	9	5.56	50.04

TOTAL COST

EV	31.60 + 33.36	= 64.96
ED	55.30 + 22.24	= 77.54
EX	3.95 + 50.04	= 53.99

BREAKEVEN ANALYSIS

Breakeven Analysis Practice Problem

Assume the following for XYZ Medical Supply Vendor:

Fixed cost = $20,000
Selling price = $1,000
Variable cost = $600

What is the breakeven point in units? in dollars? What is the contribution margin in percent? in dollars?

Breakeven Analysis Practice Problem Solution

Breakeven point in units

$$\frac{\text{Total fixed costs}}{\text{Price} - \text{Variable costs}} = \frac{\$20,000}{\$1,000 - \$600} = 50 \text{ units}$$

Breakeven point in dollars

Breakeven units x Price = 50 x $1,000 = $50,000

Contribution margin in percent

$$\frac{\text{Price} - \text{Variable costs}}{\text{Price}} = \frac{\$1,000 - \$600}{\$1,000} = .40, \text{ or } 40\%$$

Contribution margin in dollars

Price − Variable cost = $1,000 − $600 = $400

Breakeven Analysis Self-Quiz Problem

Assume the following for your facility:

Fixed cost = $10,000
Selling price = $100
Variable cost = $20

What is the breakeven point in units? in dollars? What is the contribution margin in percent? in dollars?

Breakeven point units

$$\frac{\$10000}{\$100 - \$20} = 125 \, units$$

Breakeven Point dollars

$$125 \times \$100 = \$12,500$$

Contribution margin in percent

$$\frac{100 - 20}{100} \qquad \frac{80}{100} \qquad .80 \quad or \quad 40\%$$

Contribution margin in dollars

$$100 - 20 = \$80$$

RVU Rate-Setting

RVU Rate-Setting Practice Problem

Referring to the job-order costing and activity-based costing practice problems, calculate the charges necessary to realize a 10% gain at the XYZ Reference Lab using job-order costing and a 10% gain at the XYZ Home Health Care Corporation using activity-based costing.

RVU Rate-Setting Practice Problem Solution

Using Job Order Costing (continued from the job-order costing practice problem solution)

Step 3: Calculate the cost per procedure by multiplying the cost per RVU by the RVUs in each procedure.

Procedure	Cost/RVU ($)	x RVU	=	Cost/Procedure ($)
A	24.86	1.0		24.86
B	24.86	.5		12.43
C	24.86	.5		12.43
D	24.86	1.5		37.29
E	24.86	1.0		24.86
F	24.86	1.0		24.86
G	24.86	1.5		37.29
H	24.86	1.5		37.29
I	24.86	.5		12.43
J	24.86	1.0		24.86

Step 4: Calculate the charge necessary to realize a 10% gain at the XYZ Reference Lab.

Procedure	Cost/RVU ($) + 10%		=	Charge/Procedure ($)
A	24.86	2.49		27.35
B	12.43	1.24		13.67
C	12.43	1.24		13.67
D	37.29	3.73		41.02
E	24.86	2.49		27.35
F	24.86	2.49		27.35
G	37.29	3.73		41.02
H	37.29	3.73		41.02
I	12.43	1.24		13.67
J	24.86	2.49		27.35

Using Activity-Based Costing (continued from the job-order costing practice problem solution)

Step 7: Calculate the total cost per procedure by adding the direct cost per procedure and the indirect cost per procedure.

Procedure	Direct Cost/ Procedure ($)	+	Indirect Cost/ Procedure ($)	=	Total Cost/ Procedure ($)
PT	473.76		72.30		546.06
RT	368.48		48.20		416.68
Nursing	184.24		36.15		220.39
OT	131.60		48.20		179.80

Step 8: Calculate the charge necessary to realize a 10% gain.

Procedure	Cost/Procedure ($)	+	10%	=	Charge/Procedure ($)
PT	546.06		54.61		600.67
RT	416.68		41.67		458.35
Nursing	220.39		22.04		242.43
OT	179.80		17.98		197.78

RVU Rate-Setting Self-Quiz Problem

Referring to the job-order costing and activity-based costing self-quiz problems, calculate the charges necessary to realize a 10% gain at the lab using job-order costing and a 7% gain at the wellness center using activity-based costing.

Job order	Cost/prod	+ 10%	=	Charge/procedure
A	67.94	6.79		74.73
B	53.87	5.39		59.26
Y	44.89	4.49		49.38
P	39.66	3.97		43.63
H	31.17	3.12		34.29

Activity Based Costing	Cost/prod	+ 7%	=	Charge/Procedure
EV	64.96	4.55		69.51
ED	77.54	5.43		82.97
EY	53.99	3.78		57.77

Hourly Rate-Setting

Hourly Rate-Setting Practice Problem

Using the hourly rate method of setting rates, calculate the operating room rate to recover the costs at the XYZ Ambulatory Surgery Center:

Total projected cost of operating room = $130,000
Total projected hours of use = 2,000 hours

Hourly Rate-Setting Practice Problem Solution

Total projected cost ÷ Total projected hours of use = Hourly rate

$$\$130,000 \div 2,000 = \$65$$

Hourly Rate-Setting Self-Quiz Problem

Using the hourly rate method of setting rates, calculate the oxygen therapy rate per shift to break even at your nursing home:

Total projected cost of oxygen = $600,000
Total projected hours of use = 100,000 hours
Shift = 8 hours

$$600,000 \div 100,000 = \$6 \times 8 = \$48$$

SURCHARGE RATE-SETTING

Surcharge Rate-Setting Practice Problem

Using the surcharge method of setting rates, calculate the average prescription rate for the XYZ Pharmacy to cover their costs given the following data:

Total projected cost of the pharmacy = $60,000
Projected cost of drugs billed to patient = $45,000
Average cost per prescripton = $12

Surcharge Rate-Setting Practice Problem Solution

Step 1: Total Cost − Cost of drugs = Surcharge in $

$60,000 − $45,000 = $15,000

Step 2: Surcharge in dollars ÷ Cost of drugs = Surcharge as percentage

$15,000 ÷ $45,000 = .333

Step 3: Surcharge as percentage x Average cost per prescription = Surcharge per prescription

.333 x $12 = $4

Step 4: Surcharge per prescription + Average cost per prescription = Surcharge rate

$4 + $12 = $16

Surcharge Rate-Setting Self-Quiz Problem

Using the surcharge method of setting rates, calculate the average rate to break even in your central supply given the following data:

Total projected cost of central supply = $900,000
Total projected cost of billable supplies = $750,000
Average cost per billable supply = $7

$$900,000 - 750,000 = 150,000$$

$$150,000 \div 750,000 = 0.2$$

$$7 \times .2 = 1.4$$

$$1.4 + 7 = \$8.4$$

Effective Annual Interest Rate on Short-Term Loans

Effective Annual Interest Rate on Short-Term Loans
Practice Problem

XYZ Assisted Living Center can borrow $150,000 for 1 year at 7.5%. Calculate the amount of interest they will pay using simple interest, discount interest, and add-on interest.

Effective Annual Interest Rate on Short-Term Loans Practice Problem Solution

Using simple interest

$$7.5\% = \frac{I}{\$150,000}$$

$$I = 7.5\% \times \$150,000$$

$$I = \$11,250$$

Using discount interest

$$7.5\% = \frac{I}{\$150,000 - I}$$

$$.075(\$150,000 - I) = I$$

$$\$11,250 - .075I = I$$

$$\$11,250 = 1.075I$$

$$\frac{\$11,250}{1.075} = I$$

$$\$10,465 = I$$

Using add-on interest

$$7.5\% = \frac{I}{Principal/2}$$

$$I = .075 \times \$150,000/2$$

$$I = \$5,625$$

Effective Annual Interest Rate on Short-Term Loans Self-Quiz Problem

Your daycare center can borrow $50,000 for 1 year and pay $3,625 in interest. Calculate the interest rate you will pay using simple interest, discount interest, and add-on interest.

Simple $\quad x = \dfrac{I}{50,000} \qquad x = \dfrac{3625}{50000} \qquad = 7.25\%$

Discount

$$x = \dfrac{I}{50000 - I} \qquad x = \dfrac{3625}{50000 - 3625} \qquad = \dfrac{3625}{46375} = 7.82\%$$

ADD ON

$$x = \dfrac{3625}{50000/2} \qquad x = \dfrac{3625}{25000} \qquad x = 14.5\%$$

EFFECTIVE ANNUAL INTEREST RATE ON TRADE CREDIT

Effective Annual Interest Rate on Trade Credit Practice Problem

XYZ Hospital makes a $98 purchase on the first day of the month and must pay a $2 late fee if it does not pay within the first 10 days. What is the annual interest rate if the hospital pays on day 45? on day 30? on day 11?

Effective Annual Interest Rate on Trade Credit Practice Problem Solution

On day 45

Step 1: Annual interest paid $= \dfrac{365}{35} = 10.43 \times \$2 = \$20.86$

Step 2: Amount borrowed each time = $98

Step 3: Annual interest rate $= \dfrac{\text{Annual interest paid}}{\text{Amount borrowed each time}} = \dfrac{\$20.86}{\$98.00} = 21.3\%$

On day 30

Step 1: Annual interest paid $= \dfrac{365}{20} = 18.25 \times \$2 = \$36.50$

Step 2: Amount borrowed each time = $98

Step 3: Annual interest rate $= \dfrac{\text{Annual interest paid}}{\text{Amount borrowed each time}} = \dfrac{\$36.50}{\$98.00} = 37.2\%$

On day 11

Step 1: Annual interest paid $= \dfrac{365}{1} = 365 \times \$2 = \$730$

Step 2: Amount borrowed each time = $98

Step 3: Annual interest rate $= \dfrac{\text{Annual interest paid}}{\text{Amount borrowed each time}} = \dfrac{\$730}{\$98} = 744.89\%$

Effective Annual Interest Rate on Trade Credit Self-Quiz Problem

Assume that a hospital makes $150 purchase on the first day of the month and must pay a $5 late fee if it doesn't pay within the first 15 days. What is the annual interest rate if the hospital pays on day 16? on day 30?

DAY 16

$$\frac{365}{1} = 365 \times \$5 = \$1825 / 150 = 1216.67\%$$

Day 30

$$\frac{365}{15} = 24.33 \times \$5 = 121.67 / 150 = 81.11\%$$

FUTURE VALUE

Future Value Practice Problem

XYZ Sleep Disorder Clinic invests $106,944 for 5 years to retire a debt. Assuming the clinic can invest at 7% compounded annually, how much is the debt XYZ needs to retire?

Future Value Practice Problem Solution

$$FV = PV(1 + i)^n$$

$$FV = \$106,944(1 + .07)^5$$

$$FV = \$149,994.49$$

HB 10BII solution, compounded annually

Keys	Display	Description
1 ⬤ (P/YR)	1.00	Sets compounding periods per year to 1
5 (N)	5.00	Stores the number of compounding periods (1 x 5)
7 (I/YR)	7.00	Stores the interest rate
−106,944 (PV)	−106,944	Stores the present value
(FV)	$149,994.49	Calculates the future value

Future Value Self-Quiz Problem

Your hospital wants to invest $1,000,000 at 5% compounded quarterly. How much will the investment be worth after 10 years?

INVENTORY VALUATION

Inventory Valuation Practice Problem

XYZ Central Billing Office purchased magnetic storage disks on the following dates and amounts.

	Units	Price ($)	Total ($)
January 1 beginning balance	10	15	150
March 1 purchase	30	14	420
May 1 purchase	40	14	560
July 1 purchase	10	13	130
September 1 purchase	20	12	240
November 1 purchase	10	12	120
Total	**120**		**$1,620**
Ending inventory on Dec. 31	**35**		

Using FIFO, LIFO, and weighted average, what is the ending cost of inventory?

Inventory Valuation Practice Problem Solution

FIFO (ending inventory is composed of the most recent 35 disks purchased)

	Units	Price ($)	Total ($)
November 1 costs	10	12	120
September 1 costs	20	12	240
July 1 purchase (apply 5 disks)	5	13	65
Ending inventory	**35**		**$425**
			or $12.14 per disk

LIFO (ending inventory is composed of the earliest 35 disks purchased)

	Units	Price ($)	Total ($)
January 1 costs	10	15	150
March 1 costs (apply 25 disks)	25	14	350
Ending inventory	**35**		**$500**
			or $14.29 per disk

Weighted average (ending inventory is composed of the weighted average cost per disk times the ending inventory in units)

$$\frac{\$1,620}{120} = \$13.50 \text{ per unit} \times 35 = \$472.50$$

Inventory Valuation Self-Quiz Problem

Your radiology department purchased film on the following dates and amounts:

	Units	Price ($)	Total ($)
January 1 beginning balance	10	150	1,500
July 1 purchase	10	155	1,550
December 1 purchase	20	160	3,200
Total	**40**		**$6,250**
Ending Inventory	**25**		

Using FIFO, LIFO, and weighted average, what is your ending cost of inventory?

LIFO

	units	price	total
Jan 1 cost	10	150	1500
	10	155	1550
July	5	160	800
Dec			3850 OR 154/unit

FIFO

Dec	20	160	3200
Jul	5	155	775
			3975 OR 159/unit

weighted average $\dfrac{6250}{40} = 156.25 \times$ 3906.25

ECONOMIC ORDER QUANTITY

Economic Order Quantity Practice Problem

Find the economic order quantity (EOQ) and total cost (TC), assuming the following:

Price (P) = $100
Annual demand (D) = 1,000
Order cost (O) = $10
Interest (I) = 5%
Holding cost (H) = $.50
Lag time = 5 days

$$Qe = \sqrt{\frac{2DO}{IP + 2H}}$$

$$TC = PD + \frac{D}{Q}O + (HQ + IP\frac{Q}{2})$$

Given a constant demand for the product, how many orders will be made in 1 year?

Given a constant demand and a lag time of 5 days between order and receipt, how many units will be in stock when you place an order?

Given a constant demand, how many days are between orders?

Economic Order Quantity Practice Problem Solution

EOQ = 58 units

TC = $100,346

$$\frac{1,000}{58} = 17.24 \text{ orders per year}$$

$$\frac{1,000}{365} \times 5 = 13.70 \text{ units on the shelf}$$

$$\frac{365}{17.24} = 21.17 \text{ days between orders}$$

Economic Order Quantity Self-Quiz Problem

Find the EOQ and TC, assuming the following:

P = $5
D = 20,000
O = $10
I = 10%
H = $.75

$$Qe = \sqrt{\frac{2DO}{IP + 2H}}$$

$$TC = PD + \frac{D}{Q}O + (HQ + IP\frac{Q}{2})$$

(handwritten)
$$2\frac{(20000)(10)}{40000(10)}$$
$$\frac{400000}{.5 + 1.5}$$

$$100,000 + 447.43 + 447$$

$$5(20000) + \frac{20000}{447}(10) + (.75(447)) + (.65(223.5))$$

Given a constant demand for the product, how many orders will be made in 1 year? **44.72**

Given a constant demand and a lag time of 5 days between order and receipt, how many units will be in stock when you place an order? **273.97**

Given a constant demand, how many days are between orders? **8.16**

(handwritten left margin)
$HQ + IP\frac{Q}{2}$
$.75(447.21)$
$335.41 + 111.80$
$IP\frac{Q}{2}$
$P\frac{Q}{2}$
$\frac{Q}{2}$

What is the carrying cost? **447.21**

What is the opportunity cost? **111.80**

What is the cost of the average inventory? **1118.02**

What is the volume of the average inventory? **223.601**

The hospital has only $90,000 budgeted for the product. What is the new price the hospital must negotiate with the vendor to make budget? $ **4.46**

(handwritten)
$$5 - \frac{100,894.43 - 90000}{20000}$$

$$TC = 100,894.43$$
$$EOQ = 447.21 \text{ units}$$

REORDER POINT UNDER CONDITIONS OF UNCERTAINTY

Reorder Point Under Conditions of Uncertainty Practice Problem

Find the low-cost reorder point under conditions of uncertainty given the following information:

Stock-out cost = $5.00 per item
Overstocked cost = $1.00 per item

Probability of	.10	.25	.30	.25	.10
meeting demand	100	101	102	103	104

Reorder Point Under Conditions of Uncertainty Practice Problem Solution

Reorder Point	Potential Demand					Cost ($)
	100	**101**	**102**	**103**	**104**	
Probability	.10	.25	.30	.25	.10	
100	.00	1.25	3.00	3.75	2.00	10.00
101	.10	.00	1.50	2.50	1.50	5.60
102	.20	.25	.00	1.25	1.00	2.70
103	.30	.50	.30	.00	.50	1.60
104	.40	.75	.60	.25	.00	2.00

Conclusion: The low-cost reorder point under conditions of uncertainty is 103 units at $1.60.

Reorder Point Under Conditions of Uncertainty Self-Quiz Problem

Find the low-cost reorder point under conditions of uncertainty given the following information:

Stock-out cost = $6.00 per item
Overstocked cost = $1.00 per item

Probability of		.10	.25	.30	.25	.10
meeting demand		100	101	102	103	104

Potential Demand

Reorder PT	100 .10	101 .25	102 .30	103 .25	104 .10	Cost
100	.00	1.50	3.60	4.50	2.50	12.10
101	.10	0	1.80	3.00	1.80	6.70
102	.20	.25	0	1.5	1.2	3.15
103	.30	.50	.30	0	.60	1.70
104	.40	.75	.60	.25	0	2.00

PAYBACK PERIOD

Payback Period Practice Problem

XYZ Skilled Nursing Facility wants to buy equipment for $100,000 with projected cash flows of $22,000 per year during the equipment's useful life. What is the payback period?

Payback Period Practice Problem Solution

Year	Cash Flow ($)	Cumulative Cash Flow ($)
cf_0*	(100,000)	(100,000)
cf_1	22,000	(78,000)
cf_2	22,000	(56,000)
cf_3	22,000	(34,000)
cf_4	22,000	(12,000)
cf_5	22,000	10,000

*cf_0 represents initial investment

By looking at the table, the skilled nursing facility will recover the cost of the equipment during year 5. Sometimes when comparing capital equipment requests it might be necessary to use a value more exact than whole years. To determine exactly when during year 5 the equipment will break even (assuming an even distribution of cash flows during the years), use the following formula:

$$\text{Payback period} = \text{Year before recover} + \frac{\text{Unrecovered costs at beginning of year}}{\text{Cash flow during year}}$$

$$= 4 + \frac{(\$)12,000}{(\$)22,000} = 4.55 \text{ years}$$

Payback Period Self-Quiz Problem

Your sleep disorder clinic wants to buy new software for $20,000 with projected cash flows (salary savings) of $12,000 per year during the software's useful life. What is the payback period?

$$CF_0 \quad (20000) \qquad (20000)$$
$$CF_1 \quad 12000 \qquad 10000$$
$$CF_2 \quad 12000 \qquad 2000$$

$$1 + \frac{10000}{12000} = 1.833 \text{ years}$$

PRESENT VALUE

Present Value Practice Problem

What is the present value of $50,000, discounted at 7.5% annually for 5 years?

Present Value Practice Problem Solution

$$PV = \frac{FV}{(1 + i)^n}$$

$$PV = \frac{\$\,50{,}000}{(1 + .075)^5}$$

$$PV = \frac{\$50{,}000}{1.4356}$$

$$PV = \$34{,}829$$

HB 10BII Solution, compounded annually

Keys	Display	Description
1 ⬤ (P/YR)	1.00	Sets compounding periods per year to 1
5 (N)	5.00	Stores the number of compounding periods (1 x 5)
7.5 (I/YR)	7.50	Stores the interest rate
–50,000 (FV)	–50,000	Stores the future value
(PV)	$34,827.93	Calculates the present value

Present Value Self-Quiz Problem

What is the present value of $25,000, discounted at 3.5% annually for 3 years?

$$PV = \frac{25{,}000}{(1 + .035)^3}$$

$$PV = \frac{25000}{1.1087} = 22{,}548.93$$

DISCOUNTED PAYBACK PERIOD

Discounted Payback Period Practice Problem

XYZ Skilled Nursing Facility wants to buy equipment for $100,000 with projected cash flows of $22,000 per year at 10% during the equipment's 5-year useful life. What is the discounted payback period?

Discounted Payback Period Practice Problem Solution

Year	Cash Flow ($)	Discount x Factor	=	Discounted Cash Flow ($)	Cumulative Discounted Cash Flow ($)
cf_0*	(100,000)	1.000		(100,000)	(100,000)
cf_1	22,000	.909		19,998	(80,002)
cf_2	22,000	.826		18,172	(61,830)
cf_3	22,000	.751		16,522	(45,308)
cf_4	22,000	.683		15,026	(30,282)
cf_5	22,000	.621		13,662	(16,620)

*cf_0 represents initial investment

By looking at the table, the skilled nursing facility will not recover the cost of the equipment during the equipment's 5-year useful life.

Discounted Payback Period Self-Quiz Problem

The physician's office that you manage wants to buy equipment for $15,000 with projected cash flows of $3,000 per year over the equipment's 10-year useful life. What is the discounted payback period at 10%?

Net Present Value/Internal Rate of Return

NPV/IRR Practice Problem

XYZ Skilled Nursing Facility wants to buy equipment for $100,000 with projected cash flows of $22,000 per year during the equipment's 5-year useful life. What is the net present value at 10% with a salvage value of $10,000? What is the internal rate of return?

NPV/IRR Practice Problem Solution

		Discount Rate = 10%		Step 2:	Discount Rate = 0%	
Year	Cash Flow($)	Factor	PV ($)		Factor	PV ($)
1	22,000	0.909	19,998		1.000	22,000
2	22,000	0.826	18,172		1.000	22,000
3	22,000	0.751	16,522		1.000	22,000
4	22,000	0.683	15,026		1.000	22,000
5	32,000*	0.621	19,872		1.000	32,000
	PV of cf		**89,590**			**120,000**

Step 1:

Minus investment	$100,000
Equipment NPV	($10,410)

*Includes salvage value

Step 3: $$\frac{\$120,000 - \$100,000}{\$120,000 - \$89,590} = .6577$$

Step 4: x .10 = .0658

Step 5: + % low rate = .00

equals IRR = .0658

Steps

1 Calculate the NPV by adding the PV of cf and then subtracting the investment.

2 To calculate the IRR, first determine a second discount rate. The object is to have two PVs of cf that the investment falls between. Looking at the PV of cf already calculated, $89,590, and the investment, $100,000, it is necessary to generate a second PV of cf that is *more* than $100,000. Decreasing the discount rate will produce a larger PV of cf (whereas increasing the discount rate will produce a smaller PV of cf). The discount rate is always increased or decreased in increments of 10% because the later interpolation adjusts for 10% increments.

3 When you have determined the two PV of cf columns that the investment is between, divide the PV of cf at the low discount rate minus the investment by the PV of cf at the low discount rate minus the PV of cf at the high discount rate.

4 Multiply the answer found in Step 3 by .10 to adjust for using 10% increments for the discount rate.

5 Add the lower of the two discount rates.

HB 10BII solution

Keys	Display	Description
I ⊝ (P/YR)	1.00	Sets compounding periods per year to I
−100,000 (CF$_j$)	0 CF	Enters the initial cash flow as an anuity (−)
22,000 (CF$_j$)	I CF	Enters the first cash flow
22,000 (CF$_j$)	2 CF	Enters the second cash flow
22,000 (CF$_j$)	3 CF	Enters the third cash flow
22,000 (CF$_j$)	4 CF	Enters the fourth cash flow
32,000 (CF$_j$*)	5 CF	Enters the fifth cash flow

*In the event that there is a salvage value, enter the value to the last year cash flow

Keys	Display	Description
10 (I/YR)	10.00	Stores the interest rate
(NPV)	10,393.48	Displays NPV in dollars
(IRR)	6.05	Displays IRR in percent

NPV/IRR Self-Quiz Problem

The physician's office that you manage wants to buy equipment for $20,000 with projected cash flows of $3,000 per year over the equipment's 10-year useful life. Calculate the NPV/IRR at 10%.

RATIO ANALYSIS

Ratio Analysis Practice Problem

Using the financial statements for Hopeful Hospital in Chapter 14 of the textbook, calculate the following ratios for 20X5:

Current ratio

Collection period ratio

Days cash on hand, short-term sources, ratio

Days cash on hand, all sources, ratio

Average payment period ratio

Operating margin ratio

Total margin ratio

Return on net assets ratio

Total asset turnover ratio

Age of plant ratio

Fixed asset turnover ratio

Current asset turnover ratio

Inventory ratio

Net asset financing ratio

Long-term debt capitalization ratio

Debt service coverage ratio

Cash flow to debt ratio

Ratio Analysis Practice Problem Solution

Current ratio

$$\frac{\text{Total current assets}}{\text{Total current liabilities}} = \frac{\$1,912}{\$587} = 3.26$$

Average collection period ratio

$$\frac{\text{Net receivables}}{\text{Net patient service revenue}/365} = \frac{\$1,536}{\$8,600/365} = 65.20$$

Days cash on hand, short-term sources, ratio

$$\frac{\text{Cash + Marketable securities}}{(\text{Total expenses} - \text{Depreciation expense})/365} = \frac{\$124 + \$45}{(\$9,143 - \$173)/365} = 6.88$$

Days cash on hand, all sources, ratio

$$\frac{\text{Cash + Marketable securities + Unrestricted long-term investments}}{(\text{Total expenses} - \text{Depreciation expenses})/365}$$

$$= \frac{\$124 + \$45 + \$1,010}{(\$9,143 - \$173)/365} = 47.97$$

Average payment period ratio

$$\frac{\text{Total current liabilities}}{(\text{Total expenses} - \text{Depreciation expense})/365} = \frac{\$587}{(\$9,143 - \$173)/365} = 23.88$$

Operating margin ratio

$$\frac{\text{Operating income}}{\text{Total operating revenue}} = \frac{\$90}{\$9,233} = .010$$

Total margin ratio

$$\frac{\text{Excess of revenues over expenses}}{\text{Total operating revenue}} = \frac{\$285}{\$9,233} = .031$$

Return on net assets ratio

$$\frac{\text{Excess of revenue over expenses}}{\text{Total net assets}} = \frac{\$285}{\$4,585} = .062$$

Total asset turnover ratio

$$\frac{\text{Total operating revenue} + \text{Other income}}{\text{Total assets}} = \frac{\$9,233 + \$195}{\$8,172} = 1.154$$

Age of plant ratio

$$\frac{\text{Accumulated depreciation}}{\text{Depreciation expense}} = \frac{\$1,730}{\$173} = 10.0$$

Fixed asset turnover ratio

$$\frac{\text{Total operating revenue} + \text{Other income}}{\text{Net fixed assets}} = \frac{\$9,233 + \$195}{\$5,250} = 1.796$$

Current asset turnover ratio

$$\frac{\text{Total operating revenue} + \text{Other income}}{\text{Total current assets}} = \frac{\$9,233 + \$195}{\$1,912} = 4.931$$

Inventory turnover ratio

$$\frac{\text{Total operating revenue} + \text{Other income}}{\text{Inventory}} = \frac{\$9,233 + \$195}{\$175} = 53.874$$

Net assets financing ratio

$$\frac{\text{Total net assets}}{\text{Total assets}} = \frac{\$4,585}{\$8,172} = .561$$

Long-term debt to capitalization

$$\frac{\text{Long-term debt}}{\text{Long-term debt} + \text{Net assets}} = \frac{\$3,000}{\$3,000 + \$4,585} = .396$$

Debt service coverage ratio

$$\frac{\text{Excess of revenues over expenses} + \text{Interest expense} + \text{Depreciation}}{\text{Interest} + \text{Principal payments}}$$

$$= \frac{\$285 + \$146 + \$173}{\$146 + \$400} = 1.106$$

Cash flow to debt ratio

$$\frac{\text{Excess of revenues over expenses} + \text{Depreciation}}{\text{Current liabilities} + \text{Long-term debt}}$$

$$= \frac{\$285 + \$173}{\$587 + \$3,000} = .128$$

Ratio Analysis Self-Quiz Problem

Using the financial statements for Sample Hospital in Chapter 14 of the textbook, calculate the following ratios for 20X4:

Current ratio

Average collection period ratio

Days cash on hand, short-term sources, ratio

Days cash on hand, all sources, ratio

Average payment period ratio

Operating margin ratio

Total margin ratio

Return on net assets ratio

Total asset turnover ratio

Age of plant ratio

Fixed asset turnover ratio

Current asset turnover ratio

Inventory turnover ratio

Net asset financing ratio

Long-term debt to capitalization ratio

Debt service coverage ratio

Cash flow to debt ratio

ANSWERS TO SELF-QUIZ PROBLEMS

Cost Shifting/Cost Cutting

Charge per patient to recover cost = $3,731

Amount of costs to cut = $54,650

Differential Cost Analysis

The sleep disorder program should be kept, showing a gain of $1,200,000.

Job-Order Costing

	RVU	Cost ($)
Amylase	.90	67.34
Bleeding time	.72	53.87
Uric acid	.60	44.89
Platelet count	.53	39.66
Hematocrit	.47	35.17

Activity-Based Costing

	Total Cost ($)
Evaluation	64.96
Education	77.54
Exercise	53.99

Breakeven Analysis

125 units

Breakeven point = $12,500

80%

Contribution margin = $80

RVU Rate-Setting

	Charge ($)
Amylase	74.07
Bleeding time	59.26
Uric acid	49.38
Platelet count	43.62
Hematocrit	38.69

Evaluation	69.51
Education	82.97
Exercise	57.77

Hourly-Rate Setting

Rate to break even = $48.00

Surcharge Rate-Setting

Rate to break even = $8.40

Effective Annual Interest Rate on Short-Term Loans

7.25% simple interest rate

7.82% discount interest rate

14.50% add-on interest rate

Effective Annual Interest Rate on Trade Credit

Annual interest rate of 1,216.67% on day 16

Annual interest rate of 81.10% on day 30

Future Value

Worth of investment = $1,643,619

Inventory Valuation

Ending cost of inventory:

FIFO = $3,975.

LIFO = $3,850

Weighted average = $3,906

Inventory Valuation

EOQ = 447.21 units

TC = $100,894

$$\frac{20,000}{447.21} = 44.72 \text{ orders per year}$$

$$\frac{20,000}{365} \times 5 = 273.97 \text{ units on the shelf}$$

$$\frac{365}{44.72} = 8.16 \text{ days between orders}$$

Carrying cost = $447.21

Opportunity cost = $111.80

Cost of average inventory = $1,118.02

Volume of average inventory = 223.61 units

New price to be negotiated = $4.46

Reorder Point Under Conditions of Uncertainty

Low-cost reorder point = 103 units

Payback Period

Payback period = 1.667 years

Present Value

Present value = $22,543 (formula solution)

= $22,549 (calculator solution)

Discounted Payback Period

Discounted payback period = 7.28 years

Net Present Value/Internal Rate of Return

−$1,571 NPV (formula solution)

8.642% IRR (formula solution)

−$1,566 NPV (calculator solution)

8.144% IRR (calculator solution)

Ratio Analysis

Current ratio = 2.82

Average collection period ratio = 40.61

Days cash on hand, short-term = 15.13

Days cash on hand, all sources = 40.35

Average payment period ratio = 27.32

Operating margin ratio = .003

Total margin ratio = .021

Return on net assets ratio = .042

Total asset turnover ratio = 1.19

Age of plant ratio = 9.88

Fixed asset turnover ratio = 1.78

Current asset turnover ratio = 4.79

Inventory ratio = 62.59

Net asset financing ratio = .585

Long-term debt to capitalization ratio = .3582

Debt service coverage ratio = unavailable

Cash flow to debt ratio = .114

THE CASE METHOD

OBJECTIVES

- To facilitate development of the assessment, analytical, and conceptual skills necessary for effective problem solving and decision making, as well as managerial skills associated with planning and implementing solutions

- To facilitate synthesis and integration of subject matter and application of theory to actual situations

- To encourage among students dynamic and interactive discussion that challenges their experience and values

- To provide, in a short period of time, knowledge and insights that would otherwise be gained much more slowly

INSTRUCTOR'S ROLE & RESPONSIBILITIES

- **Facilitator**—Encourage groups to think independently and to formulate and defend with sound logic and assumptions their work.

    Note: As facilitator, the instructor works with groups during the semester. This interaction in no way guarantees the correct answer or grade on the case.

- **Evaluator**—Since case study is dynamic, the criteria used in evaluating student performance is necessarily general, but takes into account the following:

  - Mastery of background information
  - Application of appropriate disciplines and analytical methodologies in the assessment component
  - Soundness of assumptions and logic
  - Degree and clarity of problems identification and articulation
  - Consistency and compatibility of assessment component with problem-solving component (e.g., degree to which recommendations and implementation plans, including method of evaluation, reflect the problems identified)
  - Presentation of material in a clear, logical manner

STUDENT'S ROLE & RESPONSIBILITIES

- **Learner**—The major responsibility for learning rests with the student in case study.

- **Participant**—The most challenging and sometimes anxiety-laden aspect of case study is the opportunity for students to present their views to others in their group. For the group to be productive, students should keep the following in mind:

  - Serious and extensive preparation by each student is critical.
  - Although student and group work should be independent, students should not hesitate to discuss the case with others.
  - During group discussions, students should expect and tolerate challenges to their views.
  - In both group discussions and the final preparation of the report, remember the importance of good communication.

CASE ANALYSIS PROCEDURE

- **Assessment component**

  - Make assumptions   — organizational objectives
                          — expectations

  - Apply disciplines   — present/past results
                          — current internal situation

  - Apply methodologies   — current external situation
                          — other factors as necessary

- **Problem-solving component**

  - Identify and describe problems
  - Formulate alternatives
  - Evaluate alternatives and make recommendation
  - Design implementation plan and method of evaluation

Source: Adapted with permission. Rakich, J. S., B. B. Longest, Jr., and K. Darr. 2004. *Cases in Health Services Management*, 4th ed. Baltimore: Health Professions Press.

Case Study: Bobcat Integrated Delivery System

Your IDS

It is December 2006, and you have just accepted the CFO position at Bobcat Integrated Delivery System (IDS). You will be reporting to Mr. Salter, Bobcat IDS chief executive officer, a retired school teacher who was hired last year. Also reporting to Mr. Salter are Mr. Wannabe, Bobcat IDS chief operating officer; Dr. Spok, Bobcat IDS medical director; and Ms. Patty Care, Bobcat IDS director of nursing. When announcing your appointment, Mr. Salter stated that your primary objective in the coming year (2007) would be to reverse the ominous financial trend which began in 2005 with an operating loss and continued in 2006. Previous operating losses were funded with investment income (investment income was $200,000 in 2006) from restricted net assets; however, your board recently passed a resolution discontinuing that practice and restricting investment income to capital expenditures.

Bobcat IDS is a not-for-profit corporation and includes a 120-bed acute care hospital, a 25-bed skilled nursing facility, a 15-bed rehab facility, a home health care agency, and an outpatient clinic. The hospital, Bobcat Community Hospital (BCH), is the only hospital in Bobcat, (name your state), a rural community of 50,000.

To acquire background information, you decide to meet with each member of the executive team first, and then meet with selected members of senior management.

Meeting with Dr. Spok

Dr. Spok, the hospital medical director, told you:

Most doctors have been on the medical staff for at least 10 years. There is little loyalty to the hospital. I and most doctors also have admitting privileges at County Hospital, a newer public hospital with better facilities 30 miles away. While it is a hassle for the doctors to drive to County Hospital to make rounds, there are few good reasons for the doctors to admit their patients to BCH. County Hospital has a hospitalist and pays physicians large amounts of money for menial service assignments like committee work (a practice that Bobcat has refused to participate in).

Meeting with Mr. Salter

Mr. Salter, chief executive officer, stated:

I just don't understand why we are losing money. I spent a considerable amount of time recruiting new doctors while keeping the existing doctors happy. The new, younger doctors just don't seem to have a sense of loyalty to BCH. Furthermore, I've tried to establish a "family atmosphere" for our employees, which stresses getting along well with others in return for job security. Everyone seems happy. Everyone except Ms. Fi Nance Myway, whom you'll be replacing. She and I both started January of 2005, and she seemed increasingly frustrated with the way I do things here—she just didn't fit in. I tried to accommodate her by implementing some of her recommendations, even though they were against my better judgment—like charging visitors for parking (generating $100,000 in other operating revenue for 2006). And when I announced that I was bringing in more business to the hospital by entering into a two-year capitated managed care agreement with the city (it expires this month)—we get $300 per month per family for taking care of the 200 city employees and their families, whether they're sick or not—Ms. Myway threw a fit at an executive team meeting. She claimed that my decisions were driving Bobcat IDS deeper into the red, and, as a result, I had to show Ms. Myway the highway for insubordination. That happened in November of 2006.

You'll be reporting to me, and I want you to do the following:

1) Using non-GAAP format, develop a 2006 statement of operations and a 2006 balance sheet (you can assume the format and numbers are correct on the 2005 balance sheet, and you can further assume that all balances carry forward to the 2006 balance sheet, with the exception of accounting for the 2006 loss from the statement of operations).

2) I need your analysis of state law (in your state) regarding our tax-exempt status. Did we provide our fair share of community benefits in 2006? Related to our non-profit tax status, I also need an analysis of the tax-exempt issue at the federal level and a detailed and current list of common hospital practices that might cause us to lose our federal tax-exempt status.

3) Many of our physicians are now admitting patients at County Hospital because County pays them for service assignments like committee work. County also provides physicians with a hospitalist. What can we do for our physicians and how much will it costs us? Please make sure you explain the typical financial arrangements with hospitalists, whether you recommend one or not.

4) Analyze the Balanced Budget Act of 1997 as it relates to Medicaid managed care. Using differential cost analysis, tell me the full cost profit/loss and the differential cost profit/loss for Bobcat IDS's 2006 Medicaid business and compare it to the following possible scenarios:

   • Things remain as is
   • We lose all our Medicaid business to County Hospital (the public facility)

- County Hospital subcontracts with us on a capitated rate (assume a similar capitated rate and utilization rate as the contract with the city—but remember, with more families!)

5) U. S. attorneys are reviewing our billing practices and physician relationships. Explain to me what they're looking for and whether you think we have any liability. What actions have been brought against hospitals like ours during the last two years? Do we need a corporate compliance plan, and, if so, what should it include? Do rural hospitals get any breaks in dealing with physicians?

6) Review current studies and literature and tell me what percent increases/decreases we can expect commercial rates, medicare rates, and medicaid rates to be over the next three years. What impact will those rate increases/decreases have on our operation?

7) Analyze my capitated managed care agreement with the city. Using differential cost analysis for 2006 data, tell me the full cost profit/loss and the differential cost profit/loss. Should we renew the contract for next year at present rates, or should we ask for a rate increase, and, if so, how much of a rate increase do we need to cover our full cost? to cover our differential cost?

8) Our radiology department is in violation of the anti-trust statutes by developing a fee schedule using RVUs developed by the radiologist's professional society. You must establish a new RVU system before we can set 2007 rates. The radiology manager has already completed some of the work and I'll send it over to you (see Table V). Please develop a hospital-specific RVU schedule and, using activity-based costing, assign 2007 radiology department rates (total radiology expenses for 2006 were $4.5 million). (Note: use technician minutes and supply expense to assign direct costs and machine minutes to assign indirect costs.)

9) Ms. Fi Nance Myway told me that financial expediency-based pricing no longer brings in much profit. Was she right? Please explain it to me in terms I can understand. If we can not cost-shift from Medicare, Medicaid, bad debt, and charity care to other payers, what are our alternatives?

10) Does our state have pricing transparency laws, and, if not, when do we expect them? Should we begin releasing pricing now in anticipation of the legislation? What should we do in preparation of either a mandated release or a voluntary release?

11) Analyze 2006's financials using ratio analysis and identify strengths, weaknesses, and recommendations for improvement.

12) Develop a 5-year strategic plan for Bobcat IDS (including benchmarked financial metrics).

13) For 2007, develop a statistical budget and then develop a revenue budget (using a financial model, determine whether to increase rates, and, if so, how much) and an expense budget in statement of operations format, including detailed footnotes explaining any changes in the numbers.

I would like to see at least four different expense scenarios:

i) Maintain expenses at 2006 levels after adjusting for volumes and mandated expenditures identified in earlier steps
i) Maintain expenses at 2006 levels after adjusting for volumes and mandated expenditures identified in earlier steps and honoring all requests (i.e., raises, additional personnel, etc)
iii) Cut expenses (from expense scenario #1) to break even in 2007
iv) Cut expenses (from expense scenario #1) to break even in 2007 and recover FY 2006 losses

14) Calculate the financial impact of buying an MRI unit that would cost $2.0 million, would have a five-year useful life, would have a 10 percent salvage value, would have a profit per procedure of $500, and would generate an estimated volume of 400 procedures per year. The bank tells me the discount rate should be 10 percent. If the project loses money, let me know how many procedures in addition to the 400 projected per year we would need to generate to break even.

15) Our long-term debt represents the remaining balance on a 30-year loan taken out 20 years ago at 11 percent with options to refinance every 10 years. If we refinance for the remaining 10 years at 7 percent, how much interest expense will we save *over the remainder of the loan?*

16) I also need your assistance in calculating the following EOQ given new data for 2007. Our inventory generally follows Pareto's Law; therefore, I have emphasized controlling those items representing the majority of our inventory activity. One of those items is IV setups. Our current situation is as follows:

2006 price	= $40
2007 projected demand	= 60,000
2007 projected ordering cost	= $25
2007 projected interest	= 6.25%
2007 projected holding cost	= $.50

The IV distributor would like to distribute a new model setup in 2007 at the same price, but is willing to reduce our carrying costs by making equal monthly deliveries. After discussing the proposal with Ms. Care, I discovered that in-service training will be required for the new model. I believe that each RN will be required to attend a two-hour seminar. I'm not quite sure where to put this training cost in the EOQ formula. Ms. Care also tells me that there are significant quality advantages with the new model, and she thinks we should order and stock the new model. What do you think? If we lose money on the new model, what price can we negotiate with the IV distributor to cover our loss?

MEETING WITH MR. OPERATOR

Mr. Operator, chief operating officer and a recent graduate from a program in healthcare administration, expressed the following concerns regarding the hospital:

It's easy to understand how we lost money last year—Mr. Salter just won't say "no" to the doctors...or the nurses, for that matter. Our revenue is down for a variety of reasons, and our expenses continue to increase. I don't know why the board ever picked a school teacher to run a healthcare system.

MEETING WITH MS. PINCHER

Ms. Penny Pincher, Bobcat IDS controller, in answer to your question regarding last year's loss, believes the following:

While acute care days are flat and SNF and rehab days and outpatient visits are up, our real financial problems involve our patient mix by financial class. Commercial and self-pay continue to decline and fixed payment and capitation continue to increase, and our board won't approve more than a 5 percent rate increase for 2007 (which affects collections for only commercial and managed care with discount—you need to make assumptions regarding Medicare and Medicaid collections).

2006 Collection/discharge

	Acute	SNF	Rehab	Home	ER	Out
Medicare	2,800	2,000	4,000	70	175	95
Medicaid	2,400	2,150	4,150	60	170	90
Private insurance	4,800	2,600	5,000	125	200	100
Managed care w/ 20% discount*	3,840	2,080	4,000	100	160	80
Managed care w/ capitation**						

*Managed care contracts with discounts call for an additional 1% discount for every 1% increase in rates.

**Managed care contract with capitation includes only the agreement with the city.

Meeting with Ms. Care

Ms. Patty Care, director of nursing, seeks your support in the following proposal:

While our financial loss is serious—most of it is attributable to low rates—we need to increase our rates to reflect our quality services. Our nurses are overworked and underpaid. I've been working on two solutions that I would like your support on. First, I believe strongly in primary care nursing, and, as a result, 90 percent of the nursing staff are RNs. RNs can perform more tasks than LPNs and nursing assistants and therefore are more efficient. This can be further justified by the acuity of our patients. Using the DRG scale as a severity index, our patients are sicker than at the average hospital. However, I am having some difficulty getting the RNs to administer meds, empty bed pans, and feed patients. Therefore, I have developed a TQM program designed to convince the RNs that all their tasks are important. All RNs are required to attend five hours of TQM training each week. Even though patient days are down, I would like to hire 10 more RNs to help cover the floors when the other RNs are in training. To recruit these RNs in light of the nursing shortage, we need to increase their average hourly rate to $25.00, which is competitive with County Hospital (see Table VI-A). This, of course, would be in addition to the cost-of-living raises already announced by the personnel director. I also would like for you to include a doctorally prepared entry-level nurse in our strategic plan for 10 years from now. If physical therapy can require a doctorate for entry level, then so should we!

Meeting with Ms. Personal

Ms. Personal, personnel director, reluctantly admits the following to you:

Hospital practice in the past has been to give the employees a cost of living raise equal to the previous year's percent increase in the consumer price index. Also, historically, we have allocated 5 percent of total wages to a merit pool to be awarded to meritorious employees based on their annual evaluations. Because Mr. Salter treats the employees like family, virtually everyone gets the raise. Because of the shortage in nursing, I am recommending that all nursing personnel receive a market raise of 5 percent, in addition to the above raises, to keep us competitive.

Here is a wage comparison to the facilities that we compete with for new hires (see Table VI-A). Mr. Salter asked us not to announce raises until your financial analysis is complete (Step #11). In the event we can't give the expected raises, I need an explanation from you giving the reason.

Meeting with Mr. Materials

Mr. Materials, materials manager, reports the following information to you:

I am projecting a 3 percent increase in supply and food prices for 2007 and a 12 percent increase in drug prices. All other prices should remain constant.

TABLE I

Bobcat IDS Balance Sheet as of December 31, 2005

	2005
Assets	
Current Assets	
Cash and cash equivalents	$ 178,750
Marketable securities	1,100,500
Accounts receivable less allowances	11,250,000
Inventories at cost	3,368,000
Other current assets	992,500
Total Current Assets	16,889,750
Land and improvements	3,250,000
Buildings	36,485,750
Fixed equipment	8,063,250
Moveable equipment	4,466,750
Property, Plant & Equipment	52,265,750
Less accumulated depreciation	(18,080,750)
Total Property, Plant & Equipment	34,185,000
TOTAL ASSETS	**$ 51,074,750**
Liabilities and Net Assets	
Current Liabilities	
Current portion of long-term debt	$ 2,151,000
Accounts payable and accrued expenses	5,400,000
Estimated amounts due to third-party payers	1,423,750
Other current liabilities	1,500,000
Total Current Liabilities	10,474,750
Long-term debt, net of current portion	37,000,000
TOTAL LIABILITIES	47,474,750
Net Assets	
Unrestricted	2,100,000
Temporarily restricted	1,000,000
Permanently restricted	500,000
TOTAL NET ASSETS	3,600,000
TOTAL LIABILITIES AND NET ASSETS	**$ 51,074,750**

TABLE II
Bobcat IDS Actual Expenses through December 31, 2006

Wages, taxes, benefits	$ 21,000,000
Professional fees and commissions	1,500,000
Drugs	2,000,000
Medical and other supplies	2,000,000
Food	1,000,000
Purchased services	1,000,000
Repairs and maintenance	1,000,000
Utilities	1,000,000
Interest	4,019,000
Depreciation	3,500,000
TOTAL EXPENSES	**$38,019,000**

Table III

Selected Industry Financial and Productivity Ratios For "A+" Rated Hospitals

	A+ S&P Rated
Financial Ratios	
Liquidity ratios	
Current ratio	2.08
Days cash-on-hand, short-term sources	23.8
Days cash-on-hand, all sources	104.6
Accounts receivable	59.2
Capital structure ratios	
Net asset financing ratio	59.50
Debt service coverage ratio	5.14
Efficiency ratios	
Total asset turnover ratio	.90
Age of plant ratio	8.09
Fixed asset turnover ratio	1.78
Current asset turnover ratio	3.89
Inventory turnover ratio	77.85
Profitability ratios	
Operating margin	*S&P does not report*
Excess margin	3.70
Return on net assets	4.70
Operating Indicator	
Length of stay	4.41
Occupancy rate	70.59
Productivity Ratios	
Cost per adjusted discharge	$4,100
Nursing service	
Nursing hours per adjusted discharge	50.00
RNs as a percent of total nursing	32.20
LPNs as a percent of total nursing	21.70
Nursing salary expense per adjusted discharge	$313
Full-time-equivalent employees	
Per occupied bed	6.02
Per bed	3.31
Total hours per adjusted discharge	**85**
Compensation per discharge	**$2,000**

TABLE IV-A
Discharges

Service (LOS)	2002	2003	2004	2005	2006
Acute (4)	8,000	7,500	7,000	7,000	6,500
SNF (13)	130	132	134	136	138
Rehab (20)	138	140	142	144	146
Home health	30,000	25,000	20,000	15,000	15,000
Emergency	32,500	35,000	37,500	40,000	42,500
Outpatient	27,500	30,000	32,500	37,500	42,500

TABLE IV-B
Percentage of Discharges by Payer

	2002	2003	2004	2005	2006
Medicare	43	44	45	45	46
Medicaid	23	24	25	25	26
Private insurance	9	7	5	3	2
MC—discount	19	19	19	15	15
MC—capitated	0	0	0	6	6
Bad debt	3	3	3	4	4
Charity	3	3	3	2	1

TABLE IV-C
2006 Charges per Discharge

Per Discharge/Visit	Bobcat ($)	County Hospital ($)
Acute	4,800	5,200
SNF	2,600	3,250
Rehab	5,000	5,000
Home health	125	125
Emergency	200	215
Outpatient	100	110

TABLE V
Radiology Department Procedures

Procedure	Technician Minutes	Supply Expense	Machine Minutes	2006 Volume
Radiology				
Chest 2-view	14	10	10	20,000
Chest 4-view	28	20	10	15,000
Hand	5	5	5	7,000
Arm	10	10	5	4,000
Foot	5	5	5	1,000
Leg	10	10	5	6,000
Flouroscopy	30	30	15	3,000
Ultrasound				
Abdomen	15	10	10	5,000
Other	10	10	10	5,622
Nuclear Medicine				
Scan	60	30	30	2,000
CT				
Head without contrast	30	50	30	200
Head with contrast	60	75	45	300
Body without contrast	30	75	30	400
Body with contrast	60	100	45	500

TABLE VI-A

Salary Survey of Area Hospitals
Average Hourly Rates, December, 2006

Position	Bobcat ($)	County Hospital ($)
Head nurse	19.00	20.24
Staff RN	16.75	18.02
Staff LPN	13.00	13.85
Nursing assistant	10.35	10.95
Laboratory tech	16.00	17.00
Radiology tech	14.00	15.00
Food server	9.20	9.60
Housekeeper	9.40	9.80
Accountant	15.00	14.00
Clerk	10.60	10.50

TABLE VI-B

Bobcat Staffing as of December 31, 2006

Department	FTEs
Adminstration	50
Medical records	9
Dietary	35
Housekeeping	25
Linen	*
Physical plant	9
Nursing**	275
Laboratory	16
Radiology	9
Respiratory therapy	5
Physical therapy	*
Emergency department physicians	4
KG/EEG	1
TOTAL	438

*contract
**90% RNs, 10% clerks

TABLE VII

Bobcat City and County
Ad Valorem/Property Tax Schedule per $100 Assessed Value

Aquifer	.00981
County	.35510
City	.47000
ISD	1.23554
Special Roads Project	.06010
Upper Bobcat River Watershed	.02000
Your state's sales tax	____

About the Author

Michael Nowicki, M.H.A., Ed.D., FACHE, FHFMA, is professor and director of the School of Health Administration at Texas State University, where he has won numerous university awards for his teaching, research, and service. He has taught for universities in California, Indiana, Kentucky, Missouri, and New Jersey, as well as for associations such as the American College of Healthcare Executives, the Healthcare Financial Management Association, the American Hospital Association, VHA, and the Association of University Programs in Health Administration.

Prior to joining academe full time in 1986, Dr. Nowicki was director of process management in the hospital division of Humana. Dr. Nowicki has also held a variety of administrative positions at Valley Medical Center in Fresno, California; Hutzel Hospital in Detroit, Michigan; Georgetown University Medical Center in Washington, DC; and Lubbock Medical Center in Texas.

Dr. Nowicki received his doctorate in educational policy studies and evaluation from the University of Kentucky, his master's in healthcare administration from George Washington University, and his bachelor's in political science from Texas Tech University. Dr. Nowicki is board certified in healthcare management and a Fellow in the American College of Healthcare Executives, and he has served as founder and advisor of student chapters, founder and president of the Central Texas Chapter, and chair of the national Book-of-the-Year Committee. Dr. Nowicki is also board certified in healthcare financial management and a Fellow in the Healthcare Financial Management Association (HFMA), and he has served as president of the South Texas Chapter, chapter liaison representative for five-state Region 9, and as a director on the national Board of Directors (serving as chair of both the Chapter Services Council and the Council on Forums). Dr. Nowicki also served on the HFMA Board of Examiners, serving as chair in 2001.

Dr. Nowicki has presented financial management seminars to audiences worldwide, including the Russian Ministry of Health in Moscow, Russian hospital executives in Golitsyno, Estonian hospital executives in Tallin, Indonesian hospital executives visiting the University of Massachusetts, as well as numerous audiences in the United States.

In addition to four editions of *The Financial Management of Hospitals and Healthcare Organizations*, Dr. Nowicki is the author of HFMA's *Introduction to Hospital Accounting*, 5th edition, published by Health Administration Press in 2006. Dr. Nowicki is a frequent contributor to numerous journals, including *hfm* (the journal of the Healthcare Financial Management Association) and *HealthLeaders*.

Dr. Nowicki and his wife, Tracey, and children, Hannah and David, live in New Braunfels, Texas.